John Greiner

Clouded Saints
and Kinky Shadows

SurVision Books

First published in 2024 by
SurVision Books
Dublin, Ireland
Reggio di Calabria, Italy
www.survisionmagazine.com

Copyright © John Greiner, 2024

Cover art: Sheer Klein, *The Inner Outer View*. Courtesy of the artist.
www.sheerklein.com
Copyright © Sheer Klein, 2024

Design © SurVision Books, 2024

ISBN: 978-1-912963-55-3

This book is in copyright. No part of this publication may be reproduced, stored in a retrieval system, or transmitted in any form or by any means without the prior permission in writing from the publisher.

Acknowledgments

Grateful acknowledgment is made to the editors of the following, in which some of these poems, or versions of them, originally appeared:

Oddball: "A Scene in the Life of Saint Jerome"

The Room Surrealist Magazine: "In a Saint John Fashion"

#ranger: "Gallery 644," "Mother Goose," "Sardines" "A Week of Insect Suicides"

SurVision Magazine: "A Crooked Well," "No One Reads History Books," and "Walter Cronkite"

CONTENTS

A Week in the Woods	5
No One Reads History Books	6
In a Saint John Fashion	8
Babel Originator	10
Elevator Pitch	11
A Crooked Well	12
A Scene in the Life of Saint Jerome	13
A Perfect Place	14
A Week of Insect Suicides	17
Fish Sandwich	18
After the Circus is Gone	20
On the Go to Nowhere in Particular	21
Patrol	22
Walter Cronkite	23
Times Square	24
Tax Day	26
Sardines	28
Tamerlane, Another Poem	30
Mother Goose	32
Gallery 644	34
Bloody Nose	37
End	40

A Walk in the Woods

The wood smells wet
in this insignificant forest.

Another man shuffles by
with a runny nose.

All the women here have coughs.
Perhaps this is the land
of pneumonia.
Better yet, the leafy suburb
of the vale of the bubonic plague.

The coffin makers must be making
a killing in town.
It's good to have a profession
in demand during tumultuous times.

In high school the guidance counselor
wanted to get me on the undertaker track,
but I was too much of a smart aleck
for that austere profession,
so now here I am
walking naked
through the wilderness
in the rain.

No One Reads History Books

My army is out of sight,
in the bushes,
shivering beside
moldering cockroaches
that Noah couldn't reach.

I was once a sailor,
so how I ended
here is simply
the end result
of Odysseus's mismanagement.

Join up and climb a tree,
tie your boot laces
with a noose
made purposeless.
March of time.

No one reads the history books.
No one writes down noteworthy remarks.
No one is on the make.
The tasks are not met,
nor are the historical imperatives.

My army has dispersed,
taken off to the sea
where all of the ships have sunk
along with their land loving sailors.
I wade out.

In a Saint John Fashion

All the puppies that have drowned
    in the Gowanus Canal
will come back, growling,
with a naughty Cerberus envy
that will make New York a safer city
    for saints.

In a Saint John fashion I trot about,
    eyes off to the end
and when that's too far gone
I drop into the Krispy Kreme.
Fleeing the Flatiron Building
the girls in masks of better ways
    head west
where kingdom come
will inevitably come.
I follow, telling them that I know the way,
    that I'm their man
and that in my Saint John's fashion
I'll get them a bit of fame.
They're not kinky enough for my play.
They've got their crucifixes at the ready,
so I get a coffee and a crawler to go.
I need to go down on Broadway,

get so low that the Battery frenzy
sweeps me off past Staten Island.
I stop, look up and watch the slim,
       sickly clouds strip,
offering all a glimpse of the sky
       and I empty myself energetically.
My sunglasses cost me a day's light,
so I keep them clean for mornings like these.
There has to be a damsel in distress
screaming far off in Brighton Beach
or Sheepshead Bay that I can catch the train
       out to,
run up her fire escape, kiss ravenously,
       help escape and have my way with.
There has to be a Motel 8 ascension
       at the ready
       in the boroughs beyond
with gangbang boys simply standing
to the side watching with incandescent gazes
       before going up in a fiery blaze,
they being there for no better purpose than to applaud
       the immaculate before burning away.
There has to be a slander to shock
and seep its way into the Revelation
before we become dry as bone
and as erotic as dust.

Babel Originator

Tall buildings filled with fortune tellers
leave me guessing at the time
since I no longer wear a wristwatch.
I'm sure if I caught the elevator up
they'd see the landslides of my fantasies.
I grew up in a place of mud.
                Too much rain.
The weathermen were despised.
There was no reason to behave
      during the deluges.
The mothers wanted to cut down
                         on costs,
they looked forward to the drowning waves
to sweep all of their slow witted kiddies away.
I was too bright for that.
I knew there were skyscrapers
that plunged, vicious, into the sky
with the intent of Babel originators.
I knew the smiles of the language
lads and ladies who I would gladly tongue
once I climbed
                        to the top
to rip the clouds open in the sky.

Elevator Pitch

My elevator pitch
is a nose dive
down the elevator shaft
at the Hotel Angleterre
with Sergei Yesenin's
red pen in hand.
They've got some great
omelets with caviar there.
If I could come up
with anything better
I would end
as Mayakovsky
with a gun clutched.

A Crooked Well

There was a crooked well
that I was always trying
to draw water from.
I was ruined then
and had a craving
to get lost in the deep
of the sunshine
that the desert had to offer.
I wanted to get to the bottom
      of that well.
You never know
what sorts of knick knacks
that you'll find in the dark.
I'm sure that all of the pharaohs
of Egypt are there,
as well as the Spanish dancer
that I saw, years ago,
in the print on Maybelle's wall
in her place back in Brooklyn.
These days are long,
I kick around a lot of dirt
and get to the bottom of nothing.

A Scene in the Life of Saint Jerome

The gas station
in the middle of the desert
is a destination
made for saints
and since Jerry's got a grand beard
he knows it's the place for him.
Jerry's a no mirage man,
knowing where to find the next oasis
to cool your engine.
He's a saint, but no prophet
and always good for a ride.
Jerry's a straight shooter
in his Chevrolet,
not given to falling for temptations
in the Saint Anthony, Flaubert
fancy flight sort of way.
Jerry's got a full tank
and ready to go.

A Perfect Place

Because of the ignorance of the magician
I got lost
        in the second house behind the hotel
Jenny talked about the home as a repetition
of loss

        that left me longing for a suicide
        back in the bed
sleep time

in the backyard
that I faced fearfully

I've got a gait to be desired

    limp

        it catches the attention of everyone who looks away
        they pay too much attention

that's how Jenny picked me up
we were both thinking about similar things
                                      that day
thinking about the beautiful trees and the best place

        to trade a sandwich for a handful of cashew nuts
we were both big fans of free trade back in those days
I'm grateful to Jenny for the plastic containers
      that she provided for our booty

          creeping through the mental wretches
     promising pretty sureties
               we planned on finding a dive to stretch
out in and plot a tomorrow beyond the glitz and glitter of the
grand motel
where
they wouldn't let us in

no compassion for the lessers of the outer classes

           the fakir assured us he was a master magician
           who knew the way
he was appealing
to our inner apathies
which lined up in the streets in front of us

              where gas stations abound
         he disappeared
         which meant
         that he was
         proficient in his trade

that's no good to me

I tried to get Jenny to see
that the trickster was just
                    off
somewhere beyond the sea
at the end of a voyage shanghaied by personal conceits

                        that's the place that she calls home

a perfect place for a bedroom

A Week of Insect Suicides

A week of insect suicides
all the buzzing done

clear air and no mosquito bites
I revel in the ashes of the honeyed ham

the slops of a whole history
so don't talk to me about the century

shoot off your mouth with a clean scream
the dentist dreams
                    of all the holes
                    in the head

this quiet is worthy of a last winter
a stop to all the tongues feeling free
                            click clack
I watch the clock
                                tick

all the talk is of red dresses
in empty rooms windowless

the electric has been disconnected

Fish Sandwich

Knowing that her name is here,
       if nothing else,
I say a prayer for her lost heart.

The moan of the passengers
on the subway train
of distances
beyond Jamaica Bay
makes me think of Jesus
          out in the storm,
              disappointed
by all the fish that swam away.
The distances that lay awake
take me to neighborhoods
that I would have never found
if I had never jumped the turnstiles with her.
Jesus made her squirm.
Worms made her squeamish
in their loss to a greater cause.

This made Lenten Fridays
soul and stomach wrenching
               for all of us
starving for a fried fish sandwich
that she would never
         allow us to devour.

After the Circus is Gone

In the downtown
rush up
to Fulton Street,
Brooklyn.
Standing.
Underground,
High Street,
A line.
Waiting.
The Circus Roncalli
has gone away.
All that remains
is an outdated poster
on the subway train.
Robert Lax
left town
to join the circus.
Maybe I should do the same.
This,
no doubt,
will be the best idea
I will have all day.

On the Go to Nowhere in Particular

She was all smiles
on the go to nowhere
      in particular.
Airports and train stations
      waited for her,
but she passed
as the world wrapped
itself around her.

Patrol

Baudelaire did better when bored.
My ennui is stiff with no great city,
just a strut in circles trying to knock
        off the skull
while waiting for the punchout clock.
The record repeats the world.
The 7 o'clock news is a rerun.
All prophets are comics who come
out of the rotten woodwork
tossed from the carpenter's shop.
We haven't had any good entertainment
since the last doomsday
and even then no one wanted to admit
to having a kinky death fetish,
they missed out on the true fun.
I can't wait for the 7th inning to arrive
with its peanuts and crackerjacks
and we all stretch to the very limits
        of possibility
where the profane becomes ecstatic
and words on the page take up more
        than space.
My legs are about to give out.

Walter Cronkite

Tongue held tight
      in the house
      on fire.
Through the air the orgy flies depart
while the mosquitos remain
licking lust in flames,
an appropriate ending.

John F. Kennedy was shot
sixty years ago today
the children of America
have forgotten Walter Cronkite's name.

Times Square

Times Square,
someone needs you
with your
luminous schlock
and bad food.

Escape from nowhere
to get to nothing,
still lost.

I've got to get grounded
somewhere else.

Times Square,
someone needs you
like they need
the Champs-Élysées
and the canals of Venice.

Pictures of nothing
somewhere once.

Times Square,
someone needs you,
but that's not me.
I'll wait for fresh meat.
All of my photos
are out of focus, anyhow.

Tax Day

Augustine was an accountant
playing at metaphysics
on a pocket calculator.
He kept the books straight.
The candy stores of Carthage
could not have hoped
for a more prestigious son.

The child's face falls,
innocent of all of Augustine's
objections to the Iliad,
his reading pleasure ended.

So many dusty books
burned in Alexandria.

Antiquities rise in price
anticipating profits to be gained
from the sale of forgotten speeches
written in lost languages.
Deaf ears serve a purpose.
Broken baby carriages
remind me of Hannibal's
battered chariots.

All of the little ones
out and about;
one day they're crawling,
the next they're taking leaps
off of cliffs
with unobstructed views.
Infants arrive at their parents'
murder fantasies
sooner than most
pediatricians expect.

I leave the *Confessions* behind
and come upon the showgirls
opening for a sea battle
worthy of Trajan's Colosseum.
I bring them chocolates
and cuckoo clocks,
from Geneva,
that Hannibal's financial
backers left behind
before setting up shop
in unoriginal Monte Carlo
where even Christ
can't get a seat.

Sardines

Cheap motels on the Pacific coast
offer up their abandoned ashtrays
to the Varanasi dust collectors.
De Chirico's shadow chain smokes
    cigarettes
unconcerned with their demise,
dropping butts in the sand
while Ariadne slumbers.
The sardine cannery, far off,
is the reward of heaven.
In Monterrey, three men
take long drags off of Cuban
    cigars,
none of them are De Chirico
who is a pleasant shadow
in far off Carmel
and who prefers Gauloise Blondes.
Ariadne will take Fidel Castro's
phantom as a lover,
it is an inevitability,
he is intricate in all of her
sleepy fetishes where ghosts
strut about in dog collars
    and top hats.

I book passage to Lisbon
while drunk on the best
        Douro wine
I could find at the corner
        liquor store.
I will avenge murdered Magellan.
He, too, was once Ariadne's
        lover.
The sardines are said
to be far better in Portugal,
some say the best in the world.

Tamerlane, Another Poem

> *For all we live to know is known,*
> *And all we seek to keep hath flown*
> —Edgar Allan Poe

I need a bigger subject,
like Tamerlane conquering
all of Central Asia and beyond,
but this is Sunday
and I am at work.
Out in the streets
brunch has once again
left more than one generation bored
and longing for a breakfast
                or lunch
simple and pure.
The football post-season rolls on
to another Super Bowl
filled with much talked about
                commercials.
In this room
people come and go
discussing Monday,
no one is talking of Michelangelo,

who is only a vague memory
from an art history class
long forgotten.
I don't envy the Monday talkers
their Sunday
being that my Monday is now almost past,
                            pure and simple,
without Eggs Benedict and Bloody Marys.
Still, I need a bigger subject,
like Timur,
known in the west as Tamerlane,
though now,
in the west,
pretty much unknown,
not even getting the vague come and go
memory of Michelangelo.
Tamerlane,
my big subject,
forgotten as Ozymandias,
and Shelley,
and Horace Smith,
on this freezing New York City Sunday,
which is my Monday.

Mother Goose

Mother Goose
my faith is lost.
I do little more
than sit by the cupboard
with Mother Hubbard
      starving.
My shadow roams
with Wynken,
Blynken and Nod.
I fear that their
wooden shoe
has sunk to bottom
of the sea.
Without shadow
how will I find
solace in the light?
On Sundays
I visit Struwwelpeter's
      grave
where I scatter
Harriet's cinders,
longing for the far off
      cigarettes
of the sixth arrondissement

where Huysmans died.
On occasion I answer
whispers with inexact rhymes.
Mother Goose,
I have flown the coop,
      leaving
without a happily
ever after.

Gallery 644

*(Hey, Richard Brautigan, look at that Canaletto,
it's the Fourth of July)*

Sky lost in the blue room;
                clear,
not a drop of rain
in Venice,
though a doge has drowned.
It's a minor matter,
he is a footnote
in a fantasy
that historians refute.
I sift through clouds
disguised
        as Wednesday haze;
mass ends.
I'm not sure
if the weekend
should come
        or go.
I've decided to abandon
the woman looking
for Washington
wading
the Potomac

with a patriotic adamance
at the Metropolitan Museum.
She is another victim
of the American education system.
She wants to go to the food court.
and have a good look at *The Last Supper*
while having a burger and fries.
She's a real American art loving
        Jesus freak.
I can only imagine how kinky
she must be on election day,
or when the Biennale
              rolls around.
              Everywhere
              tourists
are taking pictures of themselves
              in mirrors,
the bathrooms are packed,
no one can make their way to the sinks.
I refuse to shake hands.

It's the Fourth of July
and I wish I were back
              in the blue room,
or taking a dive in the Delaware
with D.C. dreams tossed
about in the breeze.
Already I have an erotic
                      twinge.

Richard Brautigan
I've found your cowboy
Kafka hat
sitting tall on the top
of my head.

Bloody Nose

They're not worried,
so why are you
if the toilets are clogged,
the train is late,
the dog is lost,
the nose is bleeding,
the eye has a stye,
the El Greco's been scratched,
the sky is falling
and Chicken Little
has just realized
that he's going to die?
They're sitting back,
having a laugh,
watching your inelegant spin,
your tottering show,
your hunger for righteousness
that has left you starving.
You've become a crusader
for justice
without a comic book
to herald your virtue.
The game has changed.
Your eyes are swollen.

The bathroom floor is flooded,
you gag as you strut
through the muck.
The lost dog has been found
choked on a bone.
Chicken Little,
left desolate, lies dying,
on this sunny afternoon
without a cloud in sight.
El Greco is as meaningless
as his *The Revelation of St. John*
which the crowd walks by
while the conservator, bored,
and the curator, unaware
of his own caustic irrelevance,
examine a scratch on the surface.
You long for St. John to be right,
Your fervor finds fulfillment
in cheap beer
at the Trinity Pub on East 84th Street.
It's all entertainment for them.
They're not worried,
so why are you,
bit player on a paltry stage?

They've got a laugh track running
and an insurance policy
that will pay off big in the end,
setting them up
for a lustrous beyond.

End

When the earth came to the end of the line
I was looking at the opening paragraph.
It was a big laugh and I couldn't believe
that I hadn't seen it coming sooner.
The doomsday man gave me an invite
to his farewell concert, but I had to decline,
he was a complete bore
and I was looking over a four leaf clover.
When in doubt, always fall back on a cliché.
So many said that the end was inevitable
and that the sun would have to go out sooner or later.
It was a brilliant sun and it might have had a much more
romantic ending in the era of locomotives.
There's a knock at the door.
There isn't even an interesting messiah
to take me over the finish line.

Selected Poetry Titles Published by SurVision Books

Contemporary Tangential Surrealist Poetry: An Anthology
 Edited by Tony Kitt
 ISBN 978-1-912963-44-7

Invasion: An Anthology of Ukrainian Poetry about the War
 Edited by Tony Kitt
 ISBN 978-1-912963-32-4

Noelle Kocot. *Humanity*
 (New Poetics: USA)
 ISBN 978-1-9995903-0-7

Marc Vincenz. *Einstein Fledermaus*
 (New Poetics: USA)
 ISBN 978-1-912963-20-1

Helen Ivory. *Maps of the Abandoned City*
 (New Poetics: England)
 ISBN 978-1-912963-04-1

Tony Kitt. *The Magic Phlute*
 (New Poetics: Ireland)
 ISBN 978-1-912963-08-9

Clayre Benzadón. *Liminal Zenith*
 (New Poetics: USA)
 ISBN 978-1-912963-11-9

Thomas Townsley. *Tangent of Ardency*
 (New Poetics: USA)
 ISBN 978-1-912963-15-7

Mikko Harvey & Jake Bauer. *Idaho Falls*
(Winner of James Tate Poetry Prize 2018)
ISBN 978-1-912963-02-7

John Bradley. *Spontaneous Mummification*
(Winner of James Tate Poetry Prize 2019)
ISBN 978-1-912963-13-3

Charles Kell. *Pierre Mask*
(Winner of James Tate Poetry Prize 2019)
ISBN 978-1-912963-19-5

Charles Borkhuis. *Spontaneous Combustion*
(Winner of James Tate Poetry Prize 2021)
ISBN 978-1-912963-30-0

Noah Falck and Matt McBride. *Prerecorded Weather*
(Winner of James Tate Poetry Prize 2022)
ISBN 978-1-912963-39-3

Jeffrey Cyphers Wright. *Fuel for Love*
(Winner of James Tate Poetry Prize 2023)
ISBN 978-1-912963-45-4

George Kalamaras. *That Moment of Wept*
ISBN 978-1-9995903-7-6

George Kalamaras. *Through the Silk-Heavy Rains*
ISBN 978-1-912963-28-7

Guillaume Apollinaire. *Ocean of Earth: Selected Poems*
Translated from French by Matthew Geden
ISBN 978-1-912963-40-9

Order our books from http://survisionmagazine.com

www.ingramcontent.com/pod-product-compliance
Lightning Source LLC
Chambersburg PA
CBHW061307040426
42444CB00010B/2554